IN THE
SHADOW
OF
MASCULINITY

" you can be anything that
you set your mind on!"

Author

Lilian M- Duclos.

J
.

IN THE
SHADOW
OF
MASCULINITY

A Candid Love Letter to Men

Lilian Mathenge-Dudek

To order additional copies of this book, contact:
Xlibris
844-714-8691
www.Xlibris.com
Orders@Xlibris.com
837103

CONTENTS

APPRECIATION

To all men who allowed me to use their life-changing stories and interactions as a way to inspire others into the need for male vulnerability. Hats off!

For the men who contributed to very touching opinions on the worldview of masculinity. Your opinions count!

To my incredible husband, David Dudek, for being my strong pillar and fundamental support during the process of writing this book. Thank you!

DEDICATION

To all men out there trying hard to fit in, in the world.

For the man suppressing his emotions and for any man that has been pressured by society to conform. For all men chained by rigid society gender traditions, to that man who has long felt "not man enough" because society expected you to give more than you could. And for that man still stuck in a manhood box.

The time is now. Get out of the box. Loosen up. You are human like any other. Put your chin up! The world needs you.

And to my son Vincent, may you live and yearn to break any dysfunctional patterns that may hinder you from being the person you were created to be.

INTRODUCTION

Most of the dysfunctional cycles that many men live today were created in them through their parents. Some men have never had a single opportunity to learn to be great fathers. This is because the fathers were never present in their lives. The truth is that narratives can be rewritten and new cycles can be created. That pain of growing up without a father figure can be erased through forgiveness. Excuses too can be erased, and men can create new legacy for their sons. Men can vow that their sons will not experience the same pain they went through by being present in their sons' lives and being the parents they never had.

To perform a particular action, robots are programmed either by guiding or by offline programming. Most of them are programmed by being guided from one point to another point through the phases of an operation, with each point being stored in a robotic control system.

Synonymously, this is how man through socialization has been programmed. A certain script of do's and don'ts has been passed on from generation to generation and can only operate on certain lines that have been drawn, making man live in a certain box of operations that I would call robotic control system.

In this book, you will encounter such moments that call up on men and society to help "cut the code" or break the cycle by all chances possible. Our next generation of men must not be subjected to the fears of mental systems that they can be liberated from.

This book is candid in how I have expressed my feelings and opinions. Most of the concept has been directly addressed to the men in a bid to help save the next generation of manhood from stereotypes and rigid gender expectations. We have long enough seen men uphold certain attributes that are off and totally are an exhibit of unhealthy masculinity. In most cases, these men don't even know that it is unhealthy because they were born into a system that embraced certain masculinity norm, blended in and are passing the same attributes to the next generations of manhood.

Theorist Albert Bandura stated that children continually learn desirable and undesirable behavior through observational learning. That means behavior can be changed and narratives can be reformed and all that undesirable, unhealthy masculinity attributes our sons learned can be unlearned too.

With a lot of loops hanging loose on gender and equality, masculinity is a context of interest that has continued to hinder many men from being real with themselves. Man has by far been socialized to fit in a box that has added more pressure to his being.

The measure of manhood has by far been misinterpreted with physical strength, looks, biceps, success, and dominance and not with gentleness, kindness, empathy, sympathy, or love that a man can show toward others including his peers. The latter is perceived as weak and not a likely measure of total manhood.

Remember, if society is aimed at healing and helping the man step out of the box, man himself must be willing not to conform. He must be ready to be saved from his own beliefs that enslave him and be willing to let go off the common tune in his head of "being man enough" to handle and figure things out on his own. He must be open to untangle himself with the enslaving mindset that has been passed on by other men in his cycle. He must be willing to end the trail on him in order to save the future generation of men.

Personalized stories and testimonies herein of many men who triumphed through the rough stereotypes and made wrong choices but came through against all odds should be calming to the reader to denote that all is not lost! The star may look blurry now, but it's bright in the horizon.

In the Shadow of Masculinity is a global book that focuses on all men in general. The phases of this book have been written for all regardless of color, race, religion, sex preference, economic status, or geographic setting. It looks at how man himself has been limited by rigid gender expectations from exploring his full potential in very many arenas due to the perception placed on him. Looks at the beliefs that man himself has adapted and tagged along as who a total man is __masculinity box.

Every boy has the ability to stop the statistics with him, the statistics of crime, gang violence, drug use and substance abuse, incarceration, or/and being an absent father to his son(s).

If boys don't learn, men won't know.
—Douglas Wilson

DISCLAIMER: Most of the ideas penned down in this book were recorded during the era and period of creating and publishing this book. However, some thoughts and variables may change in generations to come. The text in this book can therefore be used as a comparison measure according to change of events in the future.

CHAPTER 1

BREAKING THE GENERATIONAL CYCLE

CUT THE CODE

*If you want to fly on the sky, you need to leave
the earth. If you want to move forward,
you need to let go the past that drags you down.*

—Amit Ray

I t is inevitable to say that most of the problems today being faced by our generation run down the family genealogy. Lifestyle, prosperity, poverty, character, to some extent, have been passed down to us by our forefathers. Learned and repeated patterns hang around our necks like tags. Unless they are broken, they keep repeating themselves. Ending the generational patterns (cycles) is by far standing in the gap and standing out to be unique in one's beliefs and differing those beliefs that deter us from achieving our supreme potential.

This includes untangling oneself from learned patterns, any spoken words against us and unlocking self from those beliefs that limit us.

Words are powerful weapons. Words spoken can make or destroy a whole generation. Knowingly or unknowingly, words spoken by fathers to rebuke their sons can equally hinder them from pursuing their manhood prosperity.

There is a necessity to heal from whichever cards that were played on us when we were growing up. For instance, a man who grew up without his father can heal himself by being there for his son(s). He can fight and be strong to withhold his family to completion and continuity. Such a man can vow to end the bitterness of his absent father through forgiveness and create a new pattern by being there for his son(s).

Consider this separate case scenario.

Scenario 1

On one of my favorite outings, I met a young man enjoying his evening. As a way to bring out my campaign on *boy child mentorship, we discussed* in depth various factors in that regard. John (not his real name) opened up to me that he was brought up without a father and, up to date, does not know who his father is. He pointed out that it is more of an individual's choice to make up their mind to live a fulfilled life with or without a father figure. He mentioned that he vowed to stand out and be unique enough to break the pattern that he did not choose.

My friend defied the odds and said NO to fate. Today John is in a happy family, bringing up two sons to the best of his ability. In addition, he joined our initiative on accountability mentorship as a board member and a key mentor to the boys growing up without father figures within the Seattle, Washington, area. Any young man can choose to follow this or sink into some sort of pity party all his life, or allow fate and such like circumstances to drown him into self-destructive patterns in his life.

Scenario 2

In a different setting, I met a group of young men. A debate arose, and one young man, a father and a husband in his forties, said that he suffered a lot to be where he stands in life because his father disowned him. He said that he struggled through achieving an education as well as fitting in the society. All he did was blame his father for a lot of things in life. I tell you, nobody could interrupt this man as he expressed how much he loathed his father. He is a living bitter man. He vowed that the day he will meet his father, he will make sure his father pays for it (let's pray no bullets on his poor father). This man was in his forties and still bitter, holds a grudge, and has vowed to tag along an unforgiving leash around his neck. He has chosen to live a stagnant life holding on to a grudge against a father he does not even know exists. It's a pity that his sons watch him live with this kind of rage.

More often than not, it is very difficult to forgive and honor those who have wounded us. As hard as it may seem, we need to sacrifice some of our desires not to forgo grudges for the sake of our children and the generations to come. *You show steadfast love to thousands, but you repay the guilt of fathers to their children after them, o great and mighty God whose name is Lord of hosts.* The consequences of sin from one generation are passed on to the next generation. Each generation, however, has the choice to let their natural inclination repeat the cycle or to find a better way.

The greatest of powers that God gave humans is the power of choice. We can choose to follow suit and entangle ourselves with these generational patterns or choose to break them and live a free life.

Scenario 3

Lenny (not his real name) tells the story of how his own mother sent him to a foster home. He grew up feeling empty for not getting to know who his father was. In one of his Instagram posts, he said that the two people that created him brought the most pain in his life. And this is where his cycle started, created in him through his parents. He did not have even one single opportunity to learn to be a great father. One day, he vowed to himself that he was going to give himself the only opportunity to be the father he never had. He could finally give the love he never experienced, create a new cycle. It was time to erase the pain, erase the excuses and create a new legacy. He forgave the parents he never knew and had never met!

He vowed that his son would not experience the things that he himself had suffered from. Today at the time this book is written down, 2021, this gentleman has a fifteen-year-old son and is a rising star in the motivational industry, an author, and an entrepreneur. A young man whose influence has landed him in mega social media platforms such as Good Morning America, Little Big Shots by Steve Harvey, and BET, among others. This young man has also been featured in articles like Essence and I Forbes. This is through the inspiration of his father to not sink into a pity party but to break the cycle and pass the best of life's expeditions to his son.

All it takes is the willpower and strong choice to break that generational cycle. If Lenny did not take the initiative to stand in the gap and end the pattern passed on to him by his father, there would not have been this young man blowing the social media headlines with wisdom, impacting lives and giving hope to those who need it most.

"When you let go, you create time for better things to enter your life."

Generational patterns can be broken. The continuation of wrong cards played on us can be broken. Sons can erase the pain created in them by absent fathers through forgiveness and creating new meaningful cycles in their lives. I'm more to the opinion of helping our young boys break the generational code before jumping into other areas of potential exploitation, education, career or entrepreneurship, and other establishments. Imagine how well they would feel placed later in their lives knowing that they have no generational baggage. Knowing that they have broken a generational code and are now destined to start a new cycle for them and their future relations.

Let us be vigilant in helping and encouraging our men in society who suffered this to forgo the grudge and forgive their absent fathers. Not for their fathers but for themselves and their children's sake. We can teach our children to unlearn certain things that don't open their future but, instead, stagnate them. History doesn't have to repeat itself as many say. Narratives can be changed, and legacy can be edited. It takes willpower and the choice to do so. Yes, we can.

CHAPTER 2

MAN'S OWN SAFE HAVEN?

No man is an island is a common phrase that has been used for as long as I can recall. John Donne used this metaphor to show that unlike the Islands, humans cannot live in isolation or alone. We as humans were created to coexist. This could be by far finding someone that one can share sorrows, ideas, happiness, or even fears, with.

Being afraid and uncertain in life is human. It was there from the time of creation, and it is there to date. Speaking out our fears should equally be seen as human irrespective of sex. It is recorded in history books, and even biblically. If you are familiar with Jesus Christ's period before crucifixion, He spoke and opened up to His disciples. At the dinner table during the last supper Jesus told His disciples that one among them would betray Him. [spoke it out]. Being God Himself, He would have let it pass and handled it like the God He was. He didn't wait to figure it out on His own. At some point in the scripture, we read that Jesus asked God to take the cup away from Him if it was His will. Jesus had reached a place of no return.

Most of the successful people in the world today have people or friends from whom they seek counsel. These people have identified financial and life advisors. They have learned that the route of life can get messy, rough, and therefore to avoid making bad financial mistakes and choices, they seek counsel from people who have been there and done it, or professionals in their field of interest. Some heads of states too have what some call chief advisors. That said, it is normal to seek advice, and therefore our sons need to be coached on not walking alone in time of distress or whenever they may need a life's puzzle solved.

After Samuel was announced as king by Samuel, as young as he was, God enabled him to climb the ladder of fame against King Saul. As per God's plan, young David became more famous and his star was already outshining that of the then King Saul. David learned of King Saul's intention to kill him, and this did not sit very well with him. Panic and distress got hold of young David. This is evident in the book of Psalms, where we see David calling upon God for refuge.

David was filled with distress as he negotiated with Jonathan of the intended harm that Saul had laid before him. David was filled with panic as he told his buddy Jonathan this. It was so much of a relief to realize how much of a confidant his friend Jonathan was to him [safe haven], now that he was about to save David from his own father. It was at this very time, I believe, their friendship got better and David vowed to "pay back." This scripture says he did after he got into leadership as king.

David sort a safe haven in Jonathan with whom he shared all his fears and distress about King Saul's intents to kill him. Jonathan then promised a solace to David and indeed was able to hide him from his own father. It is at this point that David felt at ease and comfortable to face each day. I could only imagine the relief young David felt, knowing that expressing his fears did not portray him as a coward or as weak. What if David felt ashamed of expressing his fears? Truth be told, his fear would have conquered him, and automatically, King Saul could have killed him.

Each and every one of us needs to find or have that one person that we can speak our fears to in times of uncertainties or distress. Their assurance to us that all will be well calms our spirit, and inner peace is found. We need to encourage our sons into finding that one person that they can trust with their fears. That one person they can speak to without fear of being judged, a confidant they can unleash their fears to. A shoulder they can lean on, as many term it. There is the need to remind our sons and the men in our lives that everyone needs a safe haven, and they are not exceptional. Remind them too that it is not cowardice to cry. Yes! Better cry a river and save a life.

Be strong, be fearless, be beautiful.
And believe that anything is possible
when you have the right people there to support you

Masculinity syndrome getting in the way of men

*"Man is never so manly as when he feels deeply, acts boldly,
and expresses himself with frankness and with fervor."*
—Benjamin Disraeli

Pete (not his real name), who works for a website that focuses on men and mental illness, states that his attempt at suicide was a result of not feeling comfortable enough to ask for help. He adds that he had emotional problems but felt that he wanted to figure it out on his own. That is, until it was too late, hence he jumped off a bridge in attempt to end his life. Luckily, he survived and today has a story to share. Out of his experience and through the website, he has been able to save other lives with this closure.

There seems to be a societal norm that makes men feel pressured to act masculine. And men who strongly wrap this around their heads find getting psychological help or opening up more negatively. That can usually result in their feelings and emotions building up without an escape valve. I used the consequences of building up emotions as "bottling up" in my book *Spark Back the Men in Them* (2018 edition), and the result of this is rupture. A more familiar example is the common carbonated soft drinks. If you close a coke soda bottle with some pop in it, shake it vigorously, and let it loose, the contents will let out an explosive mess, and chances are that anyone around will be spilled on the mess. Its more or less a synonymous setup with building up emotions and feelings within us. I emphasized in the book that it could lead to worse situations in life like depression, anxiety disorder, escape to drugs, gangs, or even to violence, as ways to vent. In a worst-case scenario, attempting or completing suicide may be seen.

It calls for more induction to boys as they grow older that their sense of being men does not disqualify them from disclosure. They need to be reminded more often of the beauty of being vulnerable and opening up to someone and allowing the other person to see them for who they really are. The authentic self—their history, their fears, their failures, their flaws, including both their good and bad experiences. And this is how they learn that getting helped is OK as a way of starting to heal, building confidence, and being able to face the universe from a better perspective. Growth to better dimensions start, and they become people who can be looked upon by other generations to come.

On the other hand, society needs to stop the unrealistic masculinity demands and expectations on our men. All men fear failure (nobody likes it anyway). This is one of the biggest bugs biting our men today. Most men fear not being wealthy (perception by society of wealth as a sign of success). Men too have a tendency of fearing not being tough enough or even being perceived smart enough. Liz Plank in her book *For the Love of Men* states how young boys learn at a tender age that men don't ask for direction. A man would rather be stuck at driving in circles than ask for directions, she adds. Many men are afraid and are ashamed of seeking help for fear of being seen as weak or stupid. Whereas in the real sense, it is not the case.

I had an encounter with a very well-known man to me. He had been trying to make it in life, but somewhere along the way, he would end up being not who he intended to be. He lost job after job but still played tough to that fact. He told me of this particular job that he lost. He really loved this job. He found it very difficult to disclose this to anyone, not even his wife. He made me understand that he was not terminated as a disciplinary action but because the company had lost a lot of business and was going bankrupt. He happened to be among those employees who had to be laid off. This guy mentioned how for almost two months he woke up to the same routine he had been used to when he was employed. He actually faked that he went to work daily. He did not disclose to anyone, including his wife, that he had lost his job. Asked why, he bluntly told me that he could not stand the shame of being "fired" and not working.

See where this is going? Already, this man was conditioned to some forces of not accepting a loss, defeat, and further playing to prove a point. He was carrying shame of something he was not in control of. (Chapter 7 of this book gives an overview of healthy masculinity uncensored.)

Dr. Brene Brown, in the article "Understanding Male Vulnerability" states that the number one shame trigger for men is being perceived as weak, something which should be scraped off our minds. As I pen this book, I keep pondering to myself, that maybe handling failure and disappointments should be a compulsory topic in schools' curriculum. Emotional intelligence ought to be a number one life skill to be inducted in the classrooms by law. Schools need to have a system that can make and polish children on failure and success handling. Why? Because failure or missing out will be part of life as they grow and become responsible people in the society.

In his book *Man Enough*, actor and author Justin Baldoni discusses intensively the different aspects of man purporting to be "enough." Using his own stories, experiences, and those of others, Justin disguises a very conflicting zone that has made many men hide in a skin that does not belong to them. He says many men want to be seen as enough—strong enough, big enough, brave enough, confident enough, privileged enough, or successful enough. I believe the list goes on and on. There is that self-proclaimed urge in most men to feel better than or enough for something in order to prove a point.

Justin brings out the confusion that he was wrapped in as teenager. He explains how he thrived in competitive sports, and at the same time he felt like he did not fit in with his teammates. Why so? He states how he was bullied, picked on, and celebrated at the same time. How he simultaneously bullied and picked on other teenagers who were younger than he was. A more likely phase for almost all teenage boys. A phase in life I guess they pick to prove who is better, to pin or intimidate someone who seems to be doing better in order to demoralize him or bring him down.

Being a teacher for many years, I observed this trend more with the boys. It did not matter how good you are, if other boys sort to pick on you and bully you for some reason they did. From cornering you to wrestling you to the ground. In many cases, the one bullied would in return pick on the youngest one and bully them. Since this is a trend that they found others doing, even those that very well knew it's wrong to bully would go ahead and do it just to fit in, just to prove a point, just to be seen as macho, just to be seen as enough.

These boys grow up knowing nothing more than that they have to pin their peers down. They grow up knowing that it's OK to just bottle the pain and pick on their mates because they were picked on. They don't develop a conscience of drawing a line and simply saying, "No, it will stop with me." Instead, they continue with the same trend to show some sort of "emotional strength."

In Kenya where I went to high school, there is a common trend of "welcome" given to students enrolling in the first year in high school, also known as form 1. Some schools call it freshman, or ninth grade, to be precise. The strangest thing is that the new students are inducted into the new class by the students who are a class higher by a rough method, mistreatments, bullying, and even silencing them. They are expected to behave in a certain way and not even speak up their minds. In some schools, it is very serious that some students would drop out of school. This trend is more rampant in boys' high schools. And in mixed high schools, it is common among boys.

In his social learning theory, Albert Bandura denotes that people or children learn best through observation, modeling, and imitating the behaviors, attitudes, and emotional reactions of others. Teaching young men to jump out of behavior that they learned through the past generations and create an atmosphere best suited for the future generation is very necessary. There is the need to help them adapt a sense of pure vulnerability. They ought to learn some facts like we are all different by nature of creation and achievements, and that it is OK not to be equal to other peers. And that it is OK to allow others to help them figure things out.

Tony Porter, an international Ted Talk speaker and author of *Breaking Out of the Man Box* in one of his talks told a story of his dad. After the burial of his teenage brother, which was two hours away from home, they got into the limousine and headed back home. Along the way, they stopped at a rest area, and all the women got out first. Tony says as soon as these women got out of the car, his dad began to cry. He says his dad had been overwhelmed by the emotions of losing his son and could not hold back anymore. Yet he could not cry in the presence of the women. He waited until such a time to let out his emotions. What startled Tony most was that at the time his dad was crying, he kept apologizing to Tony for crying in his presence and applauded him for being a brave boy for not crying. It has a long way been passed to generations. That even a dad cannot mourn his own son openly, that a man cannot mourn his wife, mom, dad, or even a friend openly. It's a sad state of the mind that man has put himself in.

CHAPTER 3

MAN WORTH OF PRIDE

YOU ARE NOT ALONE!

Walk not alone o man!
Within you is a powerful flame,
With majestic power rekindle your sight,
With exotic strength rebound to regain,
For your power only you can sing again.

Walk not alone o man!
Scatter your island around your sphere,
Share your joys and so your sorrows,
Shine within and without o man,
Smile the world is clear,
Shy away not of your distress,
For no man is an island.

Walk not alone o man!
Arise your extraordinary power within,
Arouse the comfort to be heard when you cry,

Alert on informative voices of you not being enough,
For you are enough right within you.

Walk not alone o man!
The future is bright, tonnes of hope ahead,
Truest of faith, generations hold up on you,
Today is deemed your rightful day, your day of pride,
Take great pride in you, the soldier within arise,
For your tender soul awaits your courage.

Walk not alone o man!
Your day is still young, young enough to behold,
Yield for doubt, denounce lost hopes within, and reclaim your power,
Yearn for a fulfilled life as new horizons beckon,
Years of greatness await you ahead, yes, they do!
For 'tis only today a little to care.

Walk not alone o man!
Look far beyond your fears,
Listen to the best of your inner intuitions,
Lock the lessons for a better tomorrow,
Live and love yourself in depth,
For all you need is you, to love you.

You don't have to be strong to proof a point,
You are enough when you cry still,
You are enough when you lack, more so when you allow us in,
You are enough when you express of your emotions,
You alone can leave the box and still be you.

PRINCE, WEAR YOUR CROWN

Behold your pride has come, you don't have to proof,
Bestowed upon you in creation,
Be the prince you are, for your crown is your rightful identity,
Prince, wear your crown!

This is all you have as your birth rite,
Thoughts of hope for your coming life,
Thrive far and beyond the horizon,
There comes a time to linger,
Time to declare your throne,
Time to crack the code of mental emancipation,
Prince wear your crown!

Rethink creation with ease sir,
Rightfully don't be pressured to conform,
Renounce masculinity pressure to perform,
Re-encounter your might, your peace and your territory,
Prince wear your crown!

Unapologetically wear your crown, for unsung hero lies within you,
Unveil the fear to be called weak,
Unify the spirit to rise again, from whom you were created to be,
Unlearn unnecessary codes of despair, self-hate and unforgiveness,
Prince wear your crown!

Share your little pleasure of pride,
Shine on your throne with a little dance,
Shameful triggers of pressure unleash at the door,
Shout with eager to shine, surrender and give it all,
Surest way to wear your armor,
Prince wear your crown!

Your crown of freedom and liberation,
Your liberty to jump and dance,
You alone can let go off the box,
*Your fut*ure generation of manhood is beckoning,
Yours and for your future generation to restore.

LILIAN MATHENGE DUDEK COPYRIGHT@2021

It was winter 2021, and heavy snow had fallen on that weekend and totally ruined our Valentine getaway plans. We had spent the better part of Saturday shoveling snow on our driveway. On Sunday we made a little heaven of a vacation within the house. Enjoyed the little things at hand and thanked God for the beauty of snow. To me this was a blessing in disguise. As I watched the snow through our porch door, I could not stop but write the above poems with the imagination of somebody somewhere giving up on life, or feeling like life had served them lemons.

I felt so much of a fulfillment to know that one day this rubber stump and well wishes through these poems will be read and be a source of healing even after I am long gone. I wanted to write this on the day that love was being celebrated globally. And leave a permanent mark. With a deep urge to remind the future generations of man that it is OK to be themselves, OK to break the gender stereotypes, and very OK to jump out of that box.

CHAPTER 4

MAN'S CONFINED POTENTIAL THROUGH PAIN

Your past is not your potential. In any hour
you can choose to liberate the future.

Each and every one of us has that little spark within us that can ignite and light up a big flame of hope for all. It is our responsibility to try as much as possible get this spark out of ourselves. The best way to do so is by not giving up on ourselves. It is upon us to unleash this potential to the world. Be on the move and not stop at anything. Remember our duty here on earth is to make it a better place before we hit the exit.

This is how we create legacy. Keeping this in mind, it is never too late to bring forth our potential. Remember, God delights in using unlikely candidates, the most unexpected and seemingly unqualified, to fulfill and accomplish His purpose. It does not matter what cards life has played you, not even your current standing. Your abilities and acquired qualifications are secondary to God. You can start anywhere in life and be anything that you ever dreamed of. I call this the beauty of life, full of second chances.

According to the book of law, man's first evidence of great potential was taking over the responsibility to take care of God's creation, and more so in naming each animal by their name. What a great responsibility explored. Through the guidance of God, Adam (the first created man) named each one of them making sure no animal shared a name with any other. And this ability runs down mankind to date. We have men with new inventions each day, ideas to enhance human survival tactics. We all have that innate power to explore new ideas, until we discover it. Please note that when it comes to this earthly responsibility, it entails humans of all sexes.

Whenever I get a chance, I love to tell stories of greatness. Stories that turned out extraordinary and are an inspiration to anyone in need.

Sam [not his real name] was already at the peak, giving up on life. Having tried hard to fight distressing situations that led him to a deep depression that nobody knew about. He looked around but could not find anyone to confide his distressing situation to. His world was crumbling fast, and he was losing hope of living any extra day. He narrated how the fear of being judged made him shy away from speaking about his deteriorating mental status. Luckily, help came his way after he found help through a friend that he confided to. This made him feel better about himself.

Today Sam has found hidden in him the "treasure" of counseling young men. He is an accountability partner/mentor to very many young men going through such like crisis in life. All Sam needed was a little spark of hope to make him believe in himself; then he would become an ambassador of hope to young people. The innate potential in him to make change was unleashed. He is now building a legacy that will never be forgotten even after he is long gone.

God uses broken people to do great things, especially in this culture obsessed with perception and perfection. God can use our weakness and brokenness to our advantage. We only need to be alert to discovering that which is within us.

> *There is no man living who is not capable of*
> *doing more than he thinks he can do*
>
> —Henry Ford

Archie Williams was imprisoned for life at the age of fifteen years for a rape crime he did not commit. Read that again: for a crime he did not commit! After being incarcerated for thirty-seven years, he was released on March 2019. In 2021, Archie blew the stage with his performance at the famous NBC's *America's Got Talent* Season 15. Although he missed the winning button by a whisker (being second runner-up), he showcased his power with a lot of enthusiasm that thrilled the audience. I personally admired Archie exhibit potential exploitation at its best, and it was such a thriller! Having lost thirty-seven years in prison (maybe this is half his life behind bars), at fifty-two years of age, Archie could have chosen to call himself for a pity party, sit, and whine the rest of his life. Instead, he chose to get up, dust himself off, and pick up his pieces.

It doesn't matter where you really start in life or how much time you have lost. You could have started over and over again in life. See the gem in the mud and give yourself a second chance, third, and more. As long as you have the power to breathe you can do anything and become whoever you want to become. You can change the course of your life at any time of your life. It is never too late!

If Pete (not his real name), a suicide survivor in chapter 2 of this book, did not reroute his course after the suicide attempt, HeadsUpGuys would not have his worthwhile contributions that have healed many. At the time this book was penned down, according to the web, the program HeadsUpGuys had been able to reach to millions of men all over the world fighting depression. With very powerful testimonies of many of them getting help through the website. (For more information about HeadsUpGuys, go to their website, and for sure you will get out a different person. Better indeed with a lot of testimonies you can relate to.)

If you are reading this book, it is not by coincidence. You might have lived your past life full of missed opportunities, mistakes, shame, resentfulness; and your mental status seems to be failing you. Arise! Your time is now! Reroute and rekindle the fire within you. You must not punish your today with yesterday's misdoing.

I like to echo my all-time favorite international motivational speaker and author Les Brown, "Always know that as you invest in the time and efforts on you, that's the greatest ability that humans have over animals." He adds, "A dog cannot be anything but a dog, a tree cannot be anything but a tree. Human beings have got unlimited potential, you can put effort into you. And by concentrating on you and developing you, you can transform your life NO MATTER WHERE YOU ARE RIGHT NOW."

You are not alone; others have swum through deeper waters and emerged victorious. You are not exceptional. You can equally get out of it and take your life to great peaks.

When I taught in one of the schools in Kenya, Africa, we had group guidance and counseling for students each Friday before the start of the day's lessons. Our guest speaker was an enthusiastic man. Pat (not his real name) had encountered a number of students who were coming from very dysfunctional families, broken or failing families. This alone made it impossible to move to any level of mentorship. Pat would start his coaching with forgiveness and healing orientation for the students. Something I also wanted to learn from him. I vividly recall Pat sharing the ordeal he had with his biological dad when he was growing up. He opened up to the students about how his own father would treat him differently from his other siblings. This went from corporal punishments to general neglect. He gathered courage and asked his dad why he treated him as though he were not his own child. It did not sit very well with his dad.

What followed was Pat escaping and sort refuge out of his home at a tender age. He struggled his way to survival through a good Samaritan who provided his basic needs until he made his way to a neighboring country where he joined a seminary. He did not only serve in the church but also acquired a decent education. Pat did not stop at it. He forgave his father, went through a healing process, and today he is one of the best mentorship coaches I know in Kenya. In a recent TV interview, Pat said that his father turned out to be his best friend. As I pen this book down, Pat is the founder and CEO of a mentorship organization in Africa. He goes across board mentoring not only the youth but also professionals in the corporate world, the government and has become a well-known key speaker in couples' seminars. He is one of the many people I know making a great impact in helping people regain their purpose in life.

Pat chose to defy all odds and reroute his course. He did not fall into a pity party but instead chose to change the narrative and he is giving his all to coach and mentor many. Yes! *"You can transform your life no matter where you are right now"* (Les Brown). Pat knew the ball was in his court, and he played it well. The scores in his life right now must be huge. His purpose on earth can be felt by many. Patrick will leave a tangible legacy.

For precious metal to be purified, a tough process has to take place. Gold being one of the most famous and precious metal goes through refining by fire. One of the commonest and oldest way of purifying gold actually is by fire. The ore goes through a furnace with 1064 degrees centigrade heat. It is then heaped with generous amount of soda ash and borax. This then effectively separates the gold from more impurities and other traces of metal. When you look at a well-refined piece of gold, you will see your reflection on it. How about that, a mud-filled piece of ore to a reflective "mirror." The process is tough, but the results are priceless. This metaphor of gold and our lives is the imagery that God uses.

At some point in our lives, we are like a lump of unpurified gold. With no value, ugly to the sight, and heavy with impurities; problems, lack, failures, discontent, disease, discouragements, unforgiveness, childhood tremors, rejection, loss of all kinds, and so forth. One thing I have a strong belief in is that God will never leave us in such a state. We are His image, and He wants us to look at our lives and see His reflection. Suffering is not His reflection and in one way or another, He will get us out of it.

If you are going through life's rough terrains right now hang in there. Hold tight and don't lose the grip. When the time is ripe, the Lord will make everything new. *"He has made everything beautiful in its time. He has also set eternity in the human heart; Yet no one can fathom what God has done from the beginning to end"* (Eccles. 3:11, NIV).

Psalms 139 is a sure bet of how God thinks well of us. Verses 13 through 17 summarize God's knowledge of our existence before we were even formed in our mothers' wombs to who we are today. The Lord claims us as His children. That said, He will never leave us. All we need to do is trust in Him and do good. Remember always that we are the Lord's, and He created us all with a purpose to fulfill here on earth. He alone can shape us and reshape us until we are fit for His purpose and His glory.

CHAPTER 5

THE ELEPHANT IN THE ROOM

'TIS ABOUT TIME WE CONFRONT THIS MOUNTAIN

> *Staying quiet to keep the peace can be a good thing, but if the peace has already been disturbed staying quiet won't make anything better. Summon your courage and speak up when you feel the need to.*
>
> —Doe Zantamata

A QUICK DISCLOSURE CHECK

How comfortable would you be to answer the following questions up front and with honesty if you found a friend who can listen without judgment?

1. When have you felt the proudest about yourself?
2. Do you have a childhood memory good or bad?

3. If you were given a chance to face them, who is that person you would wish to forgive?

4. Who or what was the last person or thing that made you cry, and why?

5. What is your biggest fear?

Feeling at ease to answer at least three of the above questions is a powerful element of facing your fears of disclosure.

Vulnerability has been so much on the limelight, especially today in the awakening of gender equity. With many people forging forward to encourage men into opening up. As earlier mentioned, being vulnerable means allowing other people or someone else to know you fully—your thoughts, feelings, and challenges. It is more about showing your true self, your pure self whether broken or not. Just like reading a chapter in a book, you understand the context therein. Synonymously, human beings can only be well known if they open up. This is how we can get accepted, helped, and healed of our wounds. When we open up, we regain trust and feel reconnected.

On the first day that I met my husband, Dave, we sparked a connection almost immediately. He was warm, and you would say we had known each other for a lifetime. We kicked into dating a month later, and all was great. Dave spoke with so much ease, and anyone would fall in love with him. I did! We spoke endlessly on numerous topics, both on phone calls and in person. It was during one of our conversations that he opened up to me about his gambling addiction. Many years before I met him, in his youthful age, he had gambled away his life and almost everything in it. It took him acceptance of the problem that he had, and only then was he able to head his way toward recovery. He narrated this in depth of how he lost job after job in reputable organizations. He lost money, friends, and even his house was repossessed by the bank. He was declared bankrupt! He said that he felt miserable, and through the pinch of this loss, all he felt was lack of worth. He wanted to die! He took his gun, and for sure, he was ready to "end his misery." While at it, his mom was able to redirect his path.

Dave made a major U-turn in his life. Though a hard nut to crack, he had to make the decision to change, if at all he would live. He decided to quit the habit, which he did. He joined a Gamblers Anonymous (GA) program that found him a family among other addicts fighting through the journey. At the time of writing this book, Dave was many years into the program, free of gambling, and with a very strong willpower not to step back into the habit. He has not only regained what he has lost by far, but he has also become a senior mentor to other newcomers in the program fighting through addiction. To make it more appealing, Dave became a loving and caring husband to me.

Why the story, though? Just so you know, the disclosure by Dave to me while we were dating was an indication of how open he could get with whatever cards life threw at him. An attribute most women admire in men, FYI. The more he had spoken about it over the years, the more healed he felt and the more accountable he might have felt to other people. As his recipient, I would then accept him and not judge but, rather, continue reconnecting him with a safe journey he had started and doing very well in. I remember when I was writing this story, I asked him if he was OK that I put his real name on it.

He proudly said yes, adding that someone might one day read this and get a better perception of life when they get to see the person he has become today.

It called for Dave to make up his mind and ask for help. He became that purified gold for me, my son, and many more that he has helped through his life after reforming. Each one of us is a word, a step, a thought, and a decision away from getting help when we need it most. Many people have gone through tough times in life and have come out of it successfully through self-disclosure. No one is exceptional.

We have a lot of mentors today in our society. More are emerging on gender equality and healthy masculinity, among other issues on the mentorship platforms. I am convinced that more lives would be saved and more impact made if we mentors practiced what we preach to our audience. In so doing, we live the exact values we preach out there. That said, the best way to help our boys and men open up is by being vulnerable ourselves. By unmasking ourselves, we encourage them toward self-acceptance, and we teach them what unveiling our true identity is.

The pressure to break the silence is tough. This oftentimes comes because we fear to be judged. We fear that our weaknesses will be known and probably not get the help we need. But I tell you, today there is more pleasure than pressure that comes through disclosure. I have personally been there, and I know many can relate.

Were it not for me disclosing to my parents about the excessive abuse from my son's father, abuse that put my self-worth, self-esteem, and my mental health at stake, probably today I wouldn't be courageous to rubber-stamp my thoughts and opinions in books. With one time contemplating suicide, I wouldn't be here today taking care of my son, giving joy to my husband, Dave, or even encouraging someone with my writing. See, disclosure saved my life! I escaped, never to look back, and started my career at the age of thirty, fought through regaining and discovering my purpose. Today I feel more confident in myself, my decisions are solid, I speak my mind freely (how liberating), and I have learned how to build more trust over the years. I have gained a lot of positive interpersonal relationships too. I am proud I came out of a depressing situation through speaking out. Yes! Speaking out heals.

The truth is many are the times you will find yourself at a crossroads in your life as a man, and you will feel stuck. You don't know which way to take. One thing for sure—there's always a way out. All we need is to find that one person to whom we can tell it all. Allow yourself to meet that issue head-on, be frank to your listener, and experience the freedom. When this freedom comes, you start to heal and no longer feel ashamed of your past. That alone is part of healing. You will find yourself learning to ask for and actually accept help when needed. It is very liberating when, after all, you realize you are so much more than what happened to you. Much more than your losses, or even much more than your disappointments.

Apart from sharing our distress face-to-face, today there is therapy advancement, and one can get the help they need anywhere anytime. This can happen and you still remain anonymous. Many are times that one would feel ashamed to come out and speak to a physical person for various reasons. Hope is not lost, and one can start off with being anonymous.

We have the very common online helplines like the National Suicide Prevention Hotline 1-800-273-8255, the National Domestic Violence Hotline 1-800-799-7233(SAFE) or 1-800-787-3224, the Depression and Bipolar Alliance 1-800-826-3632, and the Alcohol Addiction Helpline 1-888-843-8964, among others. The above listed are numbers one can call and get help from in case of any crisis. They also have chatrooms, and help is always available because they connect you to professionals in relevance to your case.

If you know a male struggling, you can refer them to HeadsUpGuys, which is a web for men about men. In it they will find testimonies of people with a lot of different depressing ordeals and how they were able to get out of it. Celebrities included. There is no time you are alone. All you need to do is just make that one decision to let it out.

TOO SOON TO GIVE UP!

I have failed and missed opportunities in life—not at one time but many times and on several attempts. But I could bet I have not failed in life as the United States of America's sixteenth president, Abraham Lincoln, did before he became the president. Probably with the greatest example of persistence on the grounds of his failures. Many are the times I come across texts about him, and I go thinking like this guy must have a steel back.

Abraham Lincoln was born in poverty and was faced with defeat throughout his life. He failed twice in business, lost eight elections, suffered a nervous breakdown, and even lost his sweetheart. Failure had hit him so hard that he wrote a letter to his friend, "I am now the most miserable man living. If what I feel was equally distributed to the whole human family, there would not be one cheerful face on the earth."

He went ahead and ran for presidency in 1860, and he was elected the sixteenth president of the USA. He could have quit many times, but he didn't. Abraham became one of the greatest presidents in the history of the USA. If you are on the verge of drawing your last card, hold it up, don't quit. Your success story is on the way. Healing is on the way. Family restoration is on the way. You got this, and you are coming out a winner.

It will never matter who disqualifies you or thought you incompetent to undertake a certain course or task in life. You may have missed that job, that speaking engagement, or been denied access because someone thought you have nothing to offer. Relax! When the heavens open up for you and the universe conspires on your behalf, then know your hour is at hand.

To this age, the story of the greatest inventor, Thomas Edison, is told. Thomas's teachers said he was "too stupid to learn anything." He was fired from his first two jobs for being "non-productive." Today he is famous for inventing the lightbulb, having made one thousand unsuccessful attempts. Which when asked he said he did not see it as failure but saw it as an invention with one thousand steps! If you are reading this and have been written off by peers, workmates, friends, or family, put your chin up high, and know what? You got this, and your next success story is still valid. Yes, it is still too soon to give up!

In the Christian religion, we have a familiar man called Job. If there is any sort of massive loss I have heard in history, it is that of Job. Job was an extremely wealthy man. *He owned seven thousand sheep, three thousand camels, five hundred yoke of oxen, and five hundred female donkeys, and a very large number of servants.* We are told that Job lost all his animals, servants, and his children. He also got attacked by a strange disease. His friends mocked him. He was a miserable man. But not even for one moment did Job blame God even after his wife convinced him to. Due to his faithfulness, God restored him. Later, his fortune was restored. Indeed, he got twice as much as he had before.

Whenever my friend Haika and I converse, we share a lot about things happening in our lives and our families, and the story of Job becomes our point of reference and consolation. We find ourselves stating how much we are far from Job's losses and instead choose to soldier on more confidently with gratitude.

These and many more stories may be told out there, in different versions all meant to encourage someone who is at the verge of losing hope. I will say each person has their capacity of handling stress, sadness, defeat, failure, grief, and other depression triggers. The bottom line is not to let oneself go down with a depressing issue. Don't suppress it because at some point, it will "explode" you.

Look for that point of your power no matter how little may be left in you. It can still move you. That small spark of hope left in you, hold it tight and don't lose the grip. It shall be well. That situation will turn around for good. Remember recovery is always possible. Each time life gets cloudy and vision gets blurry, and you're almost clenching on your last straw, don't ever forget that you are human. Yes, you are! It is OK to have a meltdown; just don't unpack and live there. Cry it out and then refocus. It will get better because in the horizon, there is hope.

CHAPTER 6

MEN AND SUICIDE

One life lost is too many!

Though vision blurry,
And life uncertainties unfold,
I will hold you in place,
Only allow me in to share your scare,
The tune of life a little shaky,
Still, we can dance through,

Holding onto the last straw,
Don't let loose off the hook,
The horizon beckoning a promise within,
With love and hope to keep,
Behold one more chance to live.

Images of despair signal,
With little thoughts to heed,

Shun the urge to let in,
Too soon to obey,
Too soon to call it a day,

Allow me into your sphere,
Give me a portion of your worry,
Let me walk you through the pain,
The pain and the past don't define you,
For you are human first,
This pain and your past is secondary to you,

We desire the beauty of your existence,
You are relevant as you are,
Let me walk you through your dilemma,
Till dawn to linger,
For the world deserves you.

You are worthy as you are,
Allow me to walk you through your pain,
Tomorrow is brighter regardless,
With her beauty to behold,
Dare to live and let's enjoy it.

LILIAN MATHENGE DUDEK. COPYRIGHT@2021

Suicide is a complex topic with a wide range of factors that are said to contribute to it, and more so, a tragedy that leaves us with a lot of whys when someone we know completes it. Most people still think it's a sensitive topic to tackle. We all at some point in life know someone who has committed or attempted suicide. Either by relation or by association, this means that we are all highly affected, directly or indirectly, in one way or another.

That said, it is time we rise and make it a societal responsibility and own the fact that we can help ease the burden where we have the capacity to. Sadly, at the time of writing this book according to World Health Organization (WHO) in web search, suicide was declared the tenth leading cause of death in the world, with 800,000 people approximately dying from it each year. Among them, men die 3.53 times more often than women.

Though reports may not be a 100 percent clear as to why men are more likely to commit suicide than women, there are still indications denoting that men tend to commit suicide more than women do. Some state that the most valid reason is that men tend use more lethal methods when they attempt suicide, hence hard to reverse when they do. Whereas women tend to use less harmful methods which makes it easy to reverse in case discovered on time.

According to a 2000 report in *Verywell Mind*, "Understanding Suicide Among Men" written by Jerry Kennard, there has been a steady increase in the number of men who end their lives prematurely through suicide. "Although women tend to experience more suicidal thoughts, men are more likely to die by suicide," she adds.

As previously noted in my book *Spark Back the Men in Them*, society in itself piles a lot of baggage on the men with many expectations. Man is referred to as the breadwinner, provider, protector, and the key caretaker of the family. This has been almost inducted in boys from the time they are young. To such extent, man is also meant to fight for the sustenance of his family or relationships. That said, there is a lot of societal expectations placed on the man, making him feel pressured to act masculine. Even when his world is falling apart, he still wants to look *man enough*, and hence shy away from asking for help because he wants to prove that point! Not once but many times in my life I have heard some men say the common phrase: "But I am a man, I can handle it." I know you can relate. These kind of terms denote that one can figure it out on their own mean worse than good.

These little "manly beliefs" end up piling pressure, and when the men get to a point of not "handling it," and "figuring it out" alone, then the bottled pressure ruptures, and the feeling of worthlessness and hopelessness creeps in. At this point, a man may feel not worth living anymore, and hence contemplate ending his life. It is high time we take the initiative to help men and boys from a young age to open up. We need to end this male misconception. We need to encourage men to stop associating their feelings as "stress" and actually say it as it is when they feel sad or when they feel hopeless.

Correctly speaking, women, me being one of them, open up easily. We can actually open up to multiple people in search of one solution. Why so? Practically speaking, I have never heard anyone challenging a woman to be "a woman enough." May be this is the reason we women do not feel obliged or pressured to act in certain way to prove to society that we are women.

In my book *Spark Back the Men in Them*, I have strongly challenged women to also take the responsibility in helping the boys in their lives—that is, taking the personal initiative as women and mothers to speak same language where they have the chance to bring up both genders of children in their homes. This is because the language they speak to the sons or daughters become their reality. Words like "Be man enough," "Boys don't cry," "Ladies first," and "Boys will always be boys" will impact them very negatively later in life and will make them shy away from getting help when they need it most.

That said, we can agree that the buck stops at you and me! We all should own up to the responsibility to help fight with the stigma and stereotypes associated with men. The society should embrace the fact that anyone can ask for help irrespective of gender orientation. Yes, we can break the norm to conform to societal rigid traditions and gender-based expectations. We can stop the male pressure to act masculine, if at all we are to save more men from suicide. One man dying by suicide is already too many; counting to one thousand is disastrous—more than that it should be an epidemic.

It took me a lot of courage and time reading articles on suicide, more so making the decision to add this chapter in this book. I am not a psychiatrist, counselor, or researcher per se. Being an opinionated author, I felt intrigued to rubber-stamp my thoughts as I join other campaigners in the fight toward stopping or reducing the rate of suicide, more so in men.

This should not be business as usual; we have to stop terming it as a sensitive topic anymore. We must not bury our heads in the sand but instead come out and speak more about it. Normalize speaking about mental illness and seeking help where need be. Embrace the fact that men too can hurt, lack, cry, and feel hopeless. If we capture such facts, then we will destroy some cultural traditions and norms that come with nasty and rigid stereotypes about men.

I grew up in Africa, where some countries and tribes do not speak about suicide openly. Speaking about mental illness and depression is still not something one brings to the table for discussion. There are still some cultures that still believe mental illness and suicide are a result of witchcraft, and therefore not considered a priority in health, leading to little or no access to trained personnel. For this reason, Africa battles a high rate of suicide and depression according to the World Health Organization, with suicide in men rating at least three times higher than women.

There are many cases that go undocumented for fear of stigma that comes with it. In some countries like Uganda in East Africa, attempting suicide is a crime punishable by law that can lead one to a two-year jail term. Not sure how someone came up with such a law, but it was passed by the lawmakers. And unless such laws are amended, then the fight on mental health and suicide will be a tough bone to crack in such a country.

Although we have organizations that have come up with avenues to provide safe haven for people in distress in Africa, a lot still needs to be done. We must all act soon. So far in Kenya where suicide in men is on the rise compared to women, we have nongovernmental organizations that have come up and helped the community such as Befrienders Kenya, a charitable organization focusing on suicide prevention (hotline +25422178177), NISKIZE a 24-hour call center that offer face-to-face and telephone counseling sessions to special groups such as teenagers, people living with mental illness challenges, trauma, as well as suicidal thoughts (hotline 0900620800), and

Mental Wellness Kenya founded by psychologist Achieng Jahera (hotline +254717234621), among others.

We have the very common online helplines in the United States, like the National Suicide Prevention Hotline 1-800-273-8255, the National Domestic Violence Hotline 1-800-799-7233(SAFE) or 1-800-787-3224, the Depression and Bipolar Alliance 1-800-826-3632, and the Alcohol Addiction Helpline 1-888-843-8964, among others. Above listed are numbers one can call and get help in case of the crisis at hand. They also have chatrooms, and help is always available because they connect you to professionals in relevance to your case.

CHAPTER 7

HEALTHY MUSCULINITY UNSENSORED

If boys don't learn, men won't know.
—Douglas Wilson

The starring John Dutton of the show *Yellowstone* portrays what most cowboys would describe as an ultimate strength, bravery, and fierceness. His character is brought out as one most resistive to the obvious. A man who believes nothing and nobody can ever defeat him. At some point, John is diagnosed with colon cancer. He battles it alone and does not even mention a word to any of his children. He is seen asking the doctor not to disclose his health status to anyone. Until one time, while running errands in the ranch, he is in acute pain, and his son discovers that John needs immediate medical attention.

The son also discovers a scar on John's belly. John Dutton is seen telling his son that he would not like his fair share of enemies finding out that he is chronically ill. He wants to look strong even when he is on the verge of breaking down. Does this sound familiar to you?

Have you heard or seen a number of men resist going for checkup, therapy, or even decline to take medication that is prescribed because they think they are OK? Masculine norms might be the primary motivator for men's avoidance of seeking health care services. A majority of the men purport to be tough, push through pain, and don't see the need to see a doctor.

As much as society emphasizes helping men and saving them or even before we couch or talk them into vulnerability and disclosure, it is very important to get to the root cause of the problem from a young age. Unless we do so we can be sure of the re- occurrence of the same trends. That said, tackling the aspect of positive or healthy masculinity must be our topmost priority task if at all we are to see a positive change.

Healthy masculinity, or positive masculinity, as some of us may call it, has been a term I have heard used so much in this era, with society trying to induct young men into learning all about it. But really, what is this healthy masculinity? What does it entail, and maybe, which approach would be best to help men take off the mask of unhealthy masculinity?

Masculinity is an expansive term, and it will take some time, especially with older folks whose upbringing was different than most men if not all were tuned in to that traditional masculinity of "manning up theory." It's not a wonder how many men practice and express unhealthy masculinity without even realizing it.

The world may choose or have chosen to describe healthy masculinity in different ways possible. To me I sort to bring it out in its simplest form. It is when men use their physical and emotional strength to exhibit or showcase healthy behavior. Healthy behavior is anything we do that is acceptable to society, things we do with the sole intent of the better well-being of ourselves, people around us, and basically society. It is the contrast of unhealthy masculinity.

Many people out there may want to describe it on a detailed level, but it all sums up to the basics. The behavioral aspect is more of being caring, gentle, self-reliant, respectful to all people irrespective of sex orientation, being kind to people and animals, leadership, and compassion, including taking care of the environment like picking up after yourself. It is respecting all and embracing gender equality as a supplement and not viewing it as a male replacement. It is not gender insecurity.

As stated in chapter 5 of this book, it is also about being vulnerable. It is sidelining the "tough guy syndrome" and that "bad guy syndrome," "macho man," and being real. It is not being power hungry or very hungry to be labeled hero or tough. It is being truthful with yourself first. It is recognizing the fact that you can be a man and express distress as it is.

It is recognizing that males too can go through domestic violence and report the perpetrators without perceiving themselves as weak. In an article by Wendy L. Patrick, JD, PhD, on domestic violence, she stated that many male domestic violence victims suffer in silence. Men do not seek assistance due to social obstacles against them such as fear, shame, and embarrassment. Some men are afraid to report for fear of being laughed at, humiliated, or, reversely, get accused of being the abuser due to the belief that men are physically capable of fighting back when challenged. Therefore, being able to recognize that you are going through abuse as a man is a power of healthy masculinity in itself. Taking the step to blow the whistle when such times come is healthy too. As a man, you must not be convinced otherwise.

Healthy masculinity is being emotionally intelligent, which enables man to handle emotions and crisis like anger, loss, failure, disappointment, rejection, and defeat amicably. Talking of an emotionally intelligent person, honestly speaking, nothing wins in life like an emotionally intelligent man, or human being for that matter. Why? Because he will always put a limit to certain things and know how to handle emotional distress without being pressured to act otherwise.

He knows where to draw the line, respects others' boundaries, and make choices that are informed. He knows it is OK not to be dominating. In such men, the game changes, and their perception changes too. Their entire world undoubtedly changes. Note too that a man is well advanced emotionally and good for the world if he acknowledges he is wrong whenever he is and apologizes with an active change of behavior included in their intention. Not only to women but also to his peers.

When the society trains young boys on these aspects at an early age, it becomes easier for them to adapt to this fact and run with it as they grow into adults.

I came across this letter to a boy by our *little home school on Instagram* and thought it weighs an emphasis on all about healthy masculinity.

Dear little boy,

I hope you grow to know that; you can feel emotions rather than anger, crying Is not "girly," showing kindness and tenderness is not weak. You can always ask for help. You don't have to have it all together. You don't have to be aggressive or forceful to get what you want. You can be strong and tender at the same time.

COVID-19 mask-up and healthy masculinity theory

If you are still thinking, you cannot teach an old dog new tricks, read my little theory below and see how easy it can be to pick a behavior and adapt to it for survival.

When I was at the peak of writing this book, the world was in the middle of a deadly pandemic. Many people got ill, and millions died, among them politicians, poor, rich; even the religious and the laypeople were not spared by this whip. The entire world was shaken. With the pandemic came isolation, and countries had to close down in order to prevent people from getting into contact and get infected. It was a horrifying time for all. In search of hope the Center for Disease Control and Prevention (CDC) came up with the safest prevention measure as wearing a mask.

The most interesting thing is that people adapted to it so fast as a mandated CDC guideline not to allow people access into public buildings without a face mask was put in place. Most businesses went as far as declining to offer customer services unless customers had face covering on. Within a few months after the outbreak, this became the norm. Wearing a face covering was normalized as people learned to live with it. How easy it was to pick a habit and adapt to it without a problem in order to survive.

We are in an era where raising boys has become a recipe for real calamity. And a calamity it has become. Unless we act fast, we will keep destroying more men with our meaningless and unrealistic expectations as a society and recycling the same problems. On the other hand, unless men themselves rise to the occasion too and adapt to healthy masculinity, we will be mark timing on the same problems year in year out.

Just like the "mask-up phenomenon," men must normalize certain behavior like crying, going to therapy, communicating their fears, worries and sadness. Man must steer clear of the part of him that doesn't like to be wrong. Block the urge to be nasty, defensive, hide emotions, throw insults, and violence. We must as a society teach young boys to avoid shifting focus and learn how to embrace being human. We need to teach them that everybody makes mistakes in life and that it is not weakness to admit to errors made in life. It is a part of life, and honestly, it should not ignite pressure to act better.

Remember, trying to act the opposite of the current feelings is what brings forth falsehood and denial. The state of being in denial breeds unhealthy masculinity, and when the suppressed emotions cannot be held any longer, consequences become lethal.

Below is a table I clearly summarized some among many healthy vs. unhealthy masculinity characteristics that can make it easier to recognize either side of masculinity.

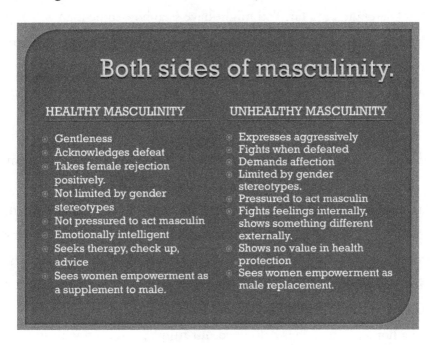

Both sides of masculinity.

HEALTHY MASCULINITY	UNHEALTHY MASCULINITY
Gentleness	Expresses aggressively
Acknowledges defeat	Fights when defeated
Takes female rejection positively.	Demands affection
Not limited by gender stereotypes	Limited by gender stereotypes.
Not pressured to act masculin	Pressured to act masculin
Emotionally intelligent	Fights feelings internally, shows something different externally.
Seeks therapy, check up, advice	Shows no value in health protection
Sees women empowerment as a supplement to male.	Sees women empowerment as male replacement.

It is more than likely that most men exhibit the above and more unhealthy masculinity attributes without realizing it. The reason is that this script was passed on from other male figures in their lives, and they fell into the trend. They have been seasoned to conform to it. But undoubtedly, the narrative can be changed; if we repeatedly emphasize to our sons, then it's easy to adapt to that which saves them and the future generation of manhood.

Saving man from himself

In chapter 5 of this book, we saw how man has been boxed in by societal expectations. Something we need to understand as much as we blame the system is that man's masculinity scares and threats come from his fellow men. How so? Man will do anything to prove that he is "man enough" in most cases to his peers. Manhood ideology has been taken too far. You might have seen how some men worship having biceps, the weights they can lift, or the model of cars they are currently driving. Man will fake his status of living standard than anything else just to fit in with his peers. Some men will get into deep debts trying to show their capability.

Some of these things are more than visible, and somehow, we hear them in our everyday life. No need for statistical research and analysis to believe what we face each day. In a bid to look successful, man will be afraid to state his financial flops openly to his peers. It's a thing in man to look "successful" and "famous" among his peers. Indeed, it's deemed as a shame to many men who cannot provide for their families. The famous old analogy of men being breadwinners in a home, to date, has colonized our minds; and even with gender equality and opportunities at our doorsteps, society is still entangled with this kind of mindset.

Far enough, man has been made to feel inadequate by his own peers. Did you know man would be humiliated more by his peers, especially in their young age (youth, to be precise) where they start to get molded for the future. They laugh and humiliate peers who cannot play the tough guy. Words such as "act like a man," "stop acting like a girl," "that's girlish," "milksop," "sissy," or worse are used on a man who cries, complains, can't play rough games or certain sports, or shows emotions openly because there is a belief among men that a real man suppresses his feelings.

What the society and men in general should learn is the lack of pressure by others to conform. Teach young boys that failure is OK as a journey of life. Refer to the story of Abraham Lincoln's broad and numerous failures. Thomas Edison with his lightbulb success story and leaving a legacy even after he had been told by his own teachers that he was too stupid to learn.

We as a society must embrace failure as a life's passage. Men need to know that it is OK not to be a breadwinner. Yes, it is. If we have all been empowered equally in the job market and economic overview, then a woman can provide for the family as much as a man can do. Let men not carry the guilt and shame of not being able to provide, especially in cases where jobs are lost or they're still pursuing an education or in unavoidable circumstances like incapacitation by all nature of disability.

Author, motivational speaker, and philanthropist Oprah Winfrey said during a Harvard commencement speech, "There is no such a thing as failure. Failure is just life trying to move us in another direction." It starts with you as a man. For a minute, let men stop blaming the system or gender equality. Start from home, that is you as a man. Change the way you perceive other men around you, either making it in various fields or not, deprived of privileges, or disadvantaged by the economic status quo or not. Be your brother's keeper because before the world saves you. You as a man must help us change this game plan. Save yourself from you!

The statistics can stop with you as a man. That son you are raising or that little boy in your neighborhood does not need to become a statistic either. Your sons or the males beneath your age must not learn the negatives that you learned while you were growing up. They must not go through the same experiences you went through while you were growing up. They must not cope with traits that leave them broken from the inside and show something different from the outside.

ALPHA MALE AND BETA MALE SYNDROME

I am more than alert, or just a little nosy, where humans mention branding names for men or other humans. One day a young friend had paid us a visit at our house. After dinner, we had a discussion on his life, and as we sped up on the nice topic on relationships, the guy mentioned how he had to show his female friend that he was hitting on then that he was an alpha male. My antennae sprung up!

There is a common male description in the socio-sexual hierarchy of dominance according to theorist Theodore Robert Beale. He describes the alpha male as that man tending to assume a dominant or have a domineering role in a social or professional situations. To some extent, the alpha male goes with a.k.a. "bad boys." Others call it "macho man."

On the other hand, the Beta male is a slang word that tends to insult (note insult) or describe a man who is seen as passive, subservient, weak and effeminate. They are perceived weak because they hate to hurt other people, therefore their passive attribute, asserts Robert. You see, man adapts to this description that one has to hurt others to be perceived strong (alpha). Sounds like some sort of animosity to me. If you read further on the human dominant hierarchy, it gives more "brands" to describe males as Omega, Sigma, Delta, and Gamma.

Personally, I find this a very vague description to use on humans. It should suit the animal kingdom perfectly because they use this to defend space where mates are concerned, defending their young ones and their food. It's a natural instinct for social dominance that animals use because they don't reason like human beings and do not have negotiation skills like we do. Therefore, using this on human beings can be very misleading and demeaning at the same time. Maybe the description could be exceptional to men at war because they are on a mandate to defend their territories no matter what. They must therefore wear the Alphas armor kind of attitude in line of duty because their core business is defense and winning at war. They have to wear a brave face even when hurt. To the men in uniform, hats off!

Remember we as human beings can have different skills and abilities. Picture this: "An Alpha in gaming community would be a Beta in a group of athletes. And an Alpha athlete is probably a Beta in a community of intellectuals where intellect is valued over physical prowess" as a good example given by *Justin Baldoni* in his book *Man Enough*. The truth is that human beings are coachable and easily adaptable to behavior; and it is absurd to put another man like you down simply because he lacks a quality that you exhibit.

I was born and raised in East Africa—in Kenya, to be precise, a country with forty-three tribes or communities, and all speak different languages. Each community has a cultural inclination that is different from another community. For instance, a man from the lake region communities is very good at fishing since this is the only economic activity he has known all his life. For survival, a man does fishing with a lot of expertise and success to provide for his family. If this same man is taken to the Maasai community where the people of the Maasai region do herding and pastoralism to feed their families and hunting using spears, he will more than likely not do well. He will be weak in that area. Very weak that he may not survive and would be described as a beta for that reason.

Man must by all means strive not to allow himself to be put down by what he cannot be. Nobody is equal to another in terms of skills and ability. Move at your own pace and only allow yourself to evolve where applicable without pressure.

By far the topic on masculinity is never conclusive and might never be. But emphasizing and repeatedly echoing these words will save a future generation of manhood. It takes effort and owning the responsibility to do so. It's up to mentors, parents, and religious leaders to take up the task to train young boys into the aspects of positive masculinity and creating a safe space for them as they grow. And teach the next generation of man the secrets of getting out of the shadow of masculinity.

MAN'S MENTAL TIME BOUND

*Success is not obtained overnight. It comes in
installments; you get a little bit today,
a little bit tomorrow until the whole package is given out.*

We are in an era that seems to teach us that time flies, and in which the young are getting themselves stuck in cycles of instant life. With a lot of information blinding the youth into chasing means that can lead to instant success. This has also been enabled by the numerous clout chasers on social media misinforming the young on how to become millionaires at the age of seventeen, eighteen, and in their twenties. It is very OK to become one at a younger age, but one thing not told for sure success is never overnight. In whichever field one opts to pursue a career—art and creativity, entrepreneurship, or education—it takes time to build. And great success even takes some substantial time to build, indeed sometimes more years than those spent in colleges.

This trend is seen at the rate in which high school graduates enroll for college. There are more girls enrolling in college as compared to young men in the US. Due to the urge to further their education, girls tend to be more knowledgeable on educational resources and are more than likely able to access these resources than the boys. This is with an exception of certain countries, especially in Africa where gender inequality in education is still an issue, where higher education still excludes many women, particularly those from marginalized communities or due to some cultural inclinations.

I recall this group of teenage boys and girls that I mentored some years back, a majority of whom were already in their high school senior year. Many are the times we mentioned what they wanted to do in college, but most boys did not really know what they wanted to do as yet. I had some parents approach me saying that they needed career mentors for their sons because their sons were already not showing interest of joining college. One particular parent even told me that her son was talking about some kind of jobs that he could do and become a millionaire without having to go to college. Well, he still did not have an idea what those jobs were when asked. This tells you the kind of misleading information out there in this regard. At the same time, a majority of the girls in the same class were already taking pre-university units in the respective courses that they were going to pursue after graduating high school.

In his findings, director and chief research scientist at Wisconsin's Equity and Inclusion Laboratory, Jerlando Jackson, pointed out that many boys beyond eighth or ninth grade perceive little benefit in college, especially considering its cost. To them college means a lot of sacrifice for a "vague payoff" in the future fueled by economic forces. In this they prefer finding odd jobs than spending four or more years in college. We know this may not be the case. Keep in mind that most of the jobs that pay a lower wage do not require more than a high school diploma, may not be very sustainable, and most of them do not have other long-term benefits.

Picture this, in the recent COVID-19 global pandemic, a lot of jobs were lost, and most people who lost jobs were those without a tertiary education. These are the majority of the people who had blue-collar jobs. Just so you know, most people who have post-secondary education or those with a college degree also packed up and went home after the lockdown. One thing is that the majority still continued to work from home and still got to be on a payroll, whereas those without a college degree did not have that luxury. This trend might have been also observed after the great recession in job creation. There was a higher job creation for those with a college degree, and those without a college degree were hit the hardest, according to Preston Cooper on a Forbes article.

In that case, the higher level of education acquired the better payoff later in life. On a larger scale, it provides more economic security.

Men tend to go for immediate or instantly gravitating chases for money. The more reason we have more young men not enrolling in college or dropping out of colleges. They want to get to that job fast, earn fast money, get to an apartment fast, or buy a great car. This is in a bid to "beat" their peers because society has trained men that to be a real man or to be man enough and respected as a man, you have to be rich. Society has perceived and measured success with wealth. Therefore, the young men want to prove a point, hence the constant rush in vain to acquire it.

This ends up being a depressing situation because the economic pressure will not permit one to acquire or exert all these with a minimum wage and within a short time. The urge for instant success can be very deceiving. It makes these young men live a masked life trying to be what they are not, or trying to prove what they are not to society, which in return hinders them from asking for help even when they need it most. It is at this point that you find most of them live a lie in a bid to boost their ego. The "man enough" phenomenon, as earlier mentioned in this book, is exhibited at this rate. More and more sensitization of our young men living true to themselves and to reality is very important if at all we are to save more men from stress, anxiety, and depression.

When reality hit, these young men end up getting stress, anxiety and escapism hence start indulgence in gangs and crime and other 'stress relieving' routes. You and I know that there is nothing like instant wealth. Phases of life cannot be skipped and the sooner our young men realize this, the better.

ROLL UP THE SLEEVE

Alone we can do so little; together we can do so much.
—Helen Keller

Community: It takes a village to raise a child. It is our profound sense of responsibility to couch the young boys as they grow up. Help them in breaking the generational patterns. This calls for the schools, sports fields, theaters, religious grounds, the home, and all other arenas that provide first hand training for children. It calls for our collective change of gender equity perception. It calls for the change in the language we use when addressing young boys because the words we used can form their reality to either worse or to good. There is that need to help them break free from the dysfunctional cycles that were created for them. It is our collective responsibility to impact how the present and the future generation of manhood will handle masculinity.

Boys: Today's boy must be willing to unlearn and break free from yesterday's lies that condition him into dysfunctional patterns. Boys must be willing to liberate themselves and their peers from gender-based fallacies that break them internally. They must be willing not to suffer emotionally and show something different externally.

There's a need for every boy to find safe spaces within their sphere to lean on in times of distress. They must seek help from safe support systems whenever they can't figure things out. Every boy has the ability to stop the statistics with him—the statistics to crime, gang violence, drug use, and substance abuse, incarceration, or/and being absent fathers to his son(s). The past is in your head; the future is in your hand. You can be barrier breakers and save many generations of future manhood.

For more recap and more insight on men and masculinity and why we need to rethink this trend, read the book *Spark Back the Men in Them* by Lilian Mathenge.

CPSIA information can be obtained
at www.ICGtesting.com
Printed in the USA
LVHW112005240622
722066LV00008B/468